Set Up a
CITY

By William Anthony

BEARPORT
PUBLISHING

Minneapolis, Minnesota

Credits

All images are courtesy of Shutterstock.com unless otherwise specified. With thanks to Getty Images, Thinkstock Photo, and iStockphoto.

Cover –Throughout, Limolida Design Studio (map paper texture), alphabe, Meilun, StockSmartStart, ideyweb, olesia_g, Denis Dubrovin, greenpic. studio, A7880S, MSSA, Elena Paletskaya, alazur, Droidworker, SIM VA (22–23 final map & map elements throughout). Cover – puruan, Sudowoodo, A7880S, robuart, KittyVector, Iryna Alex, judyjump, Boyko.Pictures, QinJin, Sean Pavone, Spiroview Inc, Flat_Enot. 4–5 – Ardea-studio, avian, Kirasolly, Alex Oakenman, MaryDesy, T photography, THINK A. 6–7 – danceyourlife, Meilun, K N, TDubov, Mr. Amarin Jitnathum, Maksim Safaniuk, Panda Vector, MaryDesy. 8–9 – Inside Creative House, Roman Babakin, Ico Maker, Andrew Rybalko, Ewelina Wachala. 10–11 – fokke baarssen, John-Kelly, ONYXprj, Andrew Krasovitckii. 12–13 – Andrew Mayovskyy, Tupungato, Macrovector, QinJin. 14–15 – Syda Productions, joyfull, Andrew Krasovitckii, leosapiens, ImageFlow. 16–17 – Tayvay, Vladimir Zhoga, CreativeMedia.org.uk. 18–19 – meunierd Photo Spirit, graficriver_icons_logo, Irina Borsuchenko. 20–21 – maradaisy, skynesher, Pressmaster. 22–23 – olllikeballoon, AuraArt, Andrew Krasovitckii.

Library of Congress Cataloging-in-Publication Data is available at www.loc.gov or upon request from the publisher.

ISBN: 978-1-63691-485-5 (hardcover)
ISBN: 978-1-63691-490-9 (paperback)
ISBN: 978-1-63691-495-4 (ebook)

For more information, write to Bearport Publishing, 5357 Penn Avenue South, Minneapolis, MN 55419. Printed in the United States of America.

Contents

How to Build Our World

Our world is amazing. It is full of places to go and things to see. There are different **environments**, from rain forests to cities. Each one has plants, animals, and more.

What does a city environment look like? Let's build one to find out!

Begin with Water

All living things need water to survive. This is why every city needs a **source** of water. For our city, let's add a river.

Big rivers might have ports. These are places where ships can bring **supplies**.

Water is moved all around a city through pipes underground. This is how people get running water in their homes.

Animals, such as ducks, live near rivers. Plants grow near the water, too.

Build the Homes

Every person needs a place to live. So, let's build some homes in our city!

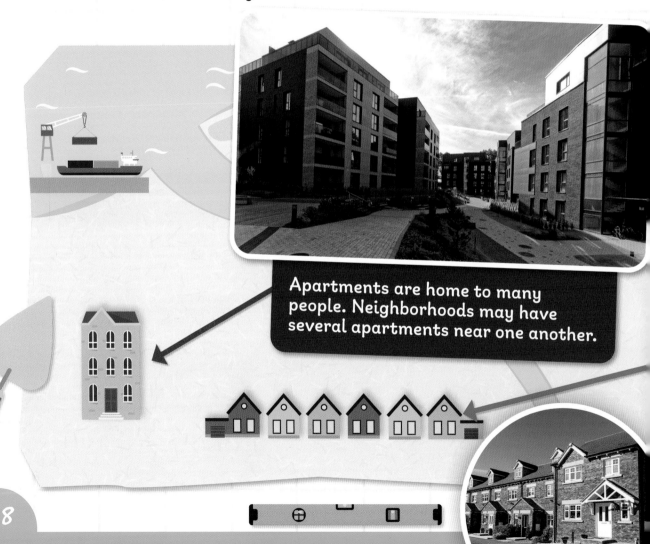

Apartments are home to many people. Neighborhoods may have several apartments near one another.

Some people live in houses. Houses can be big or small.

When people get older, they might move into a care home. These homes have nurses and other helpers.

9

Let the Electricity Flow

Anything in your home that plugs in is powered by electricity. Let's give our city some power!

We can build wind **turbines** to get electricity. Wind is a source of **energy** that will never run out.

Tall towers hold power lines high in the air. These lines carry electricity to homes.

In some cities, power lines are underground. This protects them and saves space.

Start to Travel

Now that we've got our city up and running,
how will people get from place to place?
There are many ways people can travel.

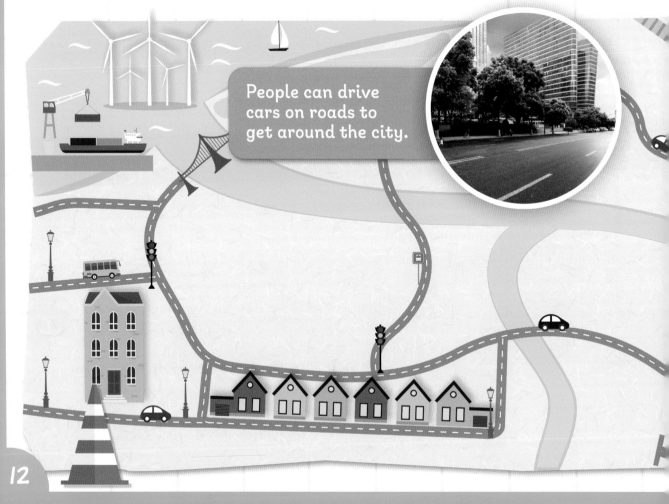

People can drive
cars on roads to
get around the city.

Trains and planes help people travel to and from cities.

Buses can move lots of people at once. They are a type of **public transportation.**

Set Up Shops and Jobs

Next, we'll add stores and places to work. People need jobs to get money so they can buy what they need.

Some people work in **offices.** Many cities have very tall office buildings called skyscrapers.

Most cities have lots of stores. There can be shops for clothes, games, and toys!

Cities also have grocery stores. Workers there help people buy food.

Add Places of Worship

People in cities believe many different things. For people who choose to follow a **religion**, let's build places to **worship**.

Muslims worship in a building called a mosque.

Hindus worship in a temple, also called a mandir.

Christians worship in a church.

17

Get Emergency Services

Next, we need people who can keep our city safe. These workers are part of the **emergency** services.

A police officer's job is to make sure people are following the law. Officers often help people in danger, too.

POLICE

The fire department puts out fires. Firefighters may also help in other emergencies.

People who are hurt or sick can go to hospitals. Nurses and doctors will help them there.

19

Place the Parks

Let's finish off our city with some parks! There, people can meet their friends and have fun.

Many parks have playgrounds for kids to enjoy.

A park may be one of the only places in a city with lots of plants and animals.

Parks help people stay healthy. Many people exercise or relax in parks.

Make Your Own Environment

City environments are incredible! They have everything people need to live, work, and enjoy life. Now, it's time for you to build your own city! You could draw it, paint it, or write about it. What do you want to put in your city?

What buildings will be in your city?

Will you add places to have fun in your city? What about a theme park or a zoo?

Every city needs a name. What will your city be called?

Glossary

emergency related to a sudden problem that must be taken care of right away

energy usable power that comes from things such as heat or wind

environments the different parts of our world in which people, animals, and plants live

offices buildings or rooms in which people work

public transportation buses, trains, and other vehicles that many people can travel on at once

religion a set of beliefs used to worship a god or gods

source where something comes from

supplies useful things, such as food or materials

turbines machines that can be turned by wind to create energy

worship a religious act where a person shows their respect for a god or gods

Index

24